Wiltshire Contiguous Parishes

GW01572166

Copyright © C E Allen & R J Thompson

Published by
CART Publications
158 Cambridge Street, Aylesbury, Bucks, HP20 1BB

First edition 1998
Reprinted 2001

ISBN 1 901824 24 1

This guide lists all parishes alphabetically with their adjoining parishes and hopefully will assist researchers to more readily organise their search patterns. Where Parishes are contiguous with other Counties these are shown using the Chapman County Codes.

FUGGLESTONE ST PETER WITH BEMERTON	South Newton; Woodford; Durnford; Stratford sub Castle; Salisbury; West Harnham; Netherhampton; Wilton
FYFIELD	Preshute; Overton; Winterbourne Bassett; Berwick Bassett
GARSDON	Charlton; Brinkworth; Lea & Cleverton; Malmesbury
GREAT BEDWIN	Little Bedwin; Shalbourne; Chute; Collingbourne Kingston; Burbage; Tidcombe; Hippenscombe; Shalbourne (BRK)
GREAT CHEVERELL	Worton and Marston; Potterne; Little Cheverell; Imber; Erlestoke
GREAT SOMERFORD	Little Somerford; Dauntsey; Christian Malford; Seagry; Stanton St Quintin; Malmesbury
GREAT WISHFORD	Stapleford; South Newton; Burcombe; Groveley Wood; Little Langford
GREY EASTON	Sherston Magna; Brokenborough; Foxley. Norton Coleparle; Shipton Moyne (GLS); Weston Birt (GLS)
GRITTLETON	Hullavington; Malmesbury; Stanton St Quintin; Leigh Delamere; Castle Combe; Littleton Drew; Alderton; Sherston Magna; Norton Coleparle; Westport St Mary
GROVELEY WOOD	Little Langford; Great Wishford; Burcombe; Barford; Baverstock;
HAM	Buttermere; Shalbourne (BRK); Inkpen (BRK)
HANKERTON	Crudwell; Minety; Charlton; Brokenborough
HANNINGTON	Castle Eaton; Highworth; Stanton Fitzwarren; Broad Blunsdon; Inglesham; Kempsford (GLS)
HARDENHUISH	Kington; Langley Burrell; Chippenham
HEDDINGTON	Calne; Bishops Cannings; Bromham; Chittoe
HEYTESBURY	Edington; Imber; Knook; Boyton; Chicklade; Pertwood; Brixton Deverill; Longbridge Deverill; Sutton Veny; Norton Bavant
HIGHWAY	Hilmarton
HIGHWORTH	Hannington; Inglesham; Sevenhampton; South Marston; Little Hinton; Wanborough; Stratton St Margaret; Stanton Fitzwarren; Buscot (BRK); Coleshill (BRK); Shrivenham (BRK)
HILL DEVERILL	Longbridge Deverill; Brixton Deverill; Maiden Bradley; Horningsham; Sutton Veny
HILMARTON	Lyneham; Cliffe Pypard; Berick Bassett; Compton Bassett; Calne; Bremhill; Berwick Bassett; Highway; Yatesbury; Cherhill
HILPERTON	Holt; Bradford on Avon; Whaddon; Semington; Steeple Ashton; Trowbridge; Staverton
HINDON	Chicklade; Fonthill Gifford; East Knoyle
HIPPENSCOMBE	Tidcombe; Chute; Great Bedwin; Collingbourne Kingston; Shalbourne (BRK)
HOLT	Bradford on Avon; Hilperton; Staverton
HOMINGTON	Britford; Odstock; Whitsbury; Combe Bissett
HORNINGSHAM	Warminster; Longbridge Deverill; Hill Deverill; Maiden Bradley; Frome (SOM)
HUISH	Overton; Wilcot; Alton Priors
HULLAVINGTON	Grittleton; Norton Coleparle; Westport St Mary; Malmesbury; Stanton St Quintin; Leigh Delamere; Castle Combe; Littleton Drew; Alderton; Sherston Magna
HUNGERFORD	Froxfield; Chilton Foliat; Ramsbury; Hungerford (BRK)

IDMISTON	Amesbury; Boscombe; Winterslow; Winterbourne Gunner; Durnford; Porton
IMBER	Erlestoke; Great Cheverell; Little Cheverell; West Lavington; Tilshead; Chitterne All Saints; Knook; Heytesbury; Edington; East Coulston
INGLESHAM	Highworth; Hannington; Kempsford (GLS); Lechlade (GLS); Buscot (BRK)
KEEVIL	Seend; Poulshot; Potterne; Worton and Marston; Erlestoke; East Coulston; Edington; Steeple Ashton; Semington
KEMBLE	Crudwell; Somerford Keynes; Poole Keynes; Oaksey; Rodmartin (GLS); Coates (GLS); Cirencester (GLS); Siddington (GLS)
KINGSTON DEVERILL	Brixton Deverill; Monkton Deverill; West Knoyle; Mere; Maiden Bradley
KINGTON	Leigh Delamere; Stanton St Quintin; Draycot Cerne; Sutton Benger; Langley Burrell; Hardenhuish; Chippenham; Yatton Keynell
KNOOK	Heytesbury; Imber; Chitterne All Saints; Upton Lovell; Boyton
LACOCK	Chippenham; Pewsham; Chittoe; Melksham; Corsham
LANDFORD	Whiteparish; Melchet Park; Plaitford; West Wellow; Bramshaw; Downton
LANGLEY BURRELL	Kington; Sutton Benger; Christian Malford; Tytherton Kellaways; Tytherton Lucas; Chippenham; Hardenhuish
LATTON	Cricklade St Sampson; Eisey; Cricklade St Mary; South Cerney (GLS); Driffield (GLS); Down Ampney (GLS)
LAVERSTOCK AND FORD	Durnford; Winterbourne Earls; Clarendon Park; Salisbury; Stratford sub Castle; Milford
LEA & CLEVERTON	Garsdon; Brinkworth; Little Somerford; Malmesbury
LEIGH DELAMERE	Grittleton; Stanton St Quintin; Kington; Yatton Keynell; Castle Combe; Hullavington
LEIGH	Ashton Keynes; Cricklade St sampson
LIDDINGTON	Stratton St Margaret; Wanborough; Aldbourne; Chisledon
LIMPLEY STOKE	Bradford on Avon; Freshford (SOM)
LITTLE HINTON	Bishopstone; Baydon; Wanborough; Highworth; Shrivenham (BRK)
LITTLE LANGFORD	Steeple Langford; Stapleford; Great Wishford; Groveley Wood; Baverstock
LITTLE CHEVERELL	Potterne; West Lavington; Imber; Great Cheverell
LITTLE BEDWIN	Ramsbury; Froxfield; Shalbourne; Great Bedwin; Burbage; Savernake; Mildenhall; Shalbourne (BRK)
LITTLE SOMERFORD	Lea & Cleverton; Brinkworth; Dauntsey; Great Somerford; Malmesbury
LITTLETON DREW	Alderton; Hullavington; Grittleton; Castle Combe; Nettleton; Luckington; Acton Turville (GLS)
LONG NEWNTON	Brokenborough; Ashley; Crudwell; Tetbury (GLS); Shipton Moyne (GLS)
LONGBRIDGE DEVERILL	Warminster; Sutton Veny; Brixton Deverill; Monkton Deverill; Horningsham
LUCKINGTON	Sopworth; Sherston Magna; Alderton; Littleton Drew; Acton Turville (GLS); Great Badminton (GLS); Hawkesbury (GLS)
LUDGERSHALL	Collingbourne Ducis; Chute Forest; North Tidworth; Chute; Appleshaw (HAM); Collingbourne Kingston; Kimpton (HAM); Fyfield (HAM)
LYDIARD TREGOZE	Lydiard Millicent; Swindon; Wroughton; Broad Hinton; Broad Town; Wootton Bassett; Brinkworth
LYDIARD MILLICENT	Purton; Rodbourne Cheney; Swindon; Lydiard Tregoze; Brinkworth
LYNEHAM	Dauntsey; Brinkworth; Tockenham; Cliffe Pypard; Hilmarton; Bremhill; Christian Malford

MADDINGTON	Chitterne All Saints; Tilshead; Orcheston St George; Shrewton; Rollstone; Winterbourne Stoke; Berwick St James; Wylye; Fisherton Delamere; Chitterne St Mary
MAIDEN BRADLEY	Horningsham; Hill Deverill; Brixton Deverill; Kingston Deverill; Mere; Marston Bigot (SOM); Witham Friary (SOM); Kilmington (SOM)
MALMESBURY	Charlton; Garsdon; Lea & Cleverton; Little Somerford; Great Somerford; Seagry; Stanton St Quintin; Grittleton; Hullavington; Westport St Mary; Brokenborough
MANNINGFORD ABBAS	Wilcot; Pewsey; Everley; Manningford Bruce;
MANNINGFORD BRUCE	Manningford Abbas; Everley; Wilsford; Woodborough; Wilcot
MARDEN	Patney; Beechingstoke; Wilsford; Chirton
MARKET LAVINGTON	Potterne; Urchfont; Wilsford; Rushall; Orcheston St George; Orcheston St Mary; Tilshead; West Lavington; Charlton
MARLBOROUGH ST PETER & ST PAUL	Preshute; Marlborough St Mary the Virgin
MARLBOROUGH ST MARY THE VIRGIN	Preshute; Mildenhall; Marlborough St Peter & St Paul
MARSTON MEYSEY	Eisey; Castle Eaton; Down Ampney (GLS); Fairford (GLS); Meysey Hampton (GLS); Kempsford (GLS)
MARTIN	Bowerchalke; Broad Chalke; Bishopstone; Stratford Tony; Combe Bissett; South Damerham; Rockbourne (HAM); Pentridge (DOR); Cranborne (DOR)
MELCHET PARK	Whiteparish; Plaitford; Landford
MELKSHAM	Lacock; Chittoe; Bromham; Rowde; Seend; Semington; Whaddon; Broughton Gifford; Atworth; Corsham
MERE	Maiden Bradley; Kingston Deverill; West Knoyle; East Knoyle; Sedgehill; Stourton; Penselwood (GLS); Bourton (DOR); Silton (DOR); Gillingham (DOR); Motcombe (DOR)
MILDENHALL	Ogbourne St Andrew; Ogbourne St George; Ramsbury; Little Bedwin; Savernake; Preshute; Marlborough St Mary the Virgin; Aldbourne
MILFORD	Stratford sub Castle; Laverstock and Ford; Salisbury
MILSTON	Figheldean; Bulford; Durrington; Figheldean; South Tidworth (HAM); Shipton Bellinger (HAM)
MILTON LILBORNE	Savernake; Wootton Rivers; Easton Royal; Collingbourne Kingston; Everley; Pewsey; Wilcot
MINETY	Oaksey; Somerford Keynes; Ashton Keynes; Cricklade St Sampson; Charlton; Hankerton; Crudwell
MONKTON DEVERILL	Brixton Deverill; Pertwood; East Knoyle; West Knoyle; Kingston Deverill
MONKTON FARLEIGH	Box; Bradford on Avon; Bathford (SOM)
NETHERAVON	Enford; Fittleton; Figheldean; Shrewton
NETHERHAMPTON	Wilton; Fugglestone St Peter with Bemerton; West Harnham; Coombe Bissett; Stratford Tony
NETTLETON	Littleton Drew; Castle Combe; North Wraxall; West Kington; Acton Turville (GLS); Tormarton (GLS)
NEWTON TONY	Amesbury; Cholderton; Allington; Boscombe; Over Wallop (HAM); Grately (HAM); Quarley (HAM)
NORTH BRADLEY	Wingfield; Bradford on Avon; Trowbridge; Steeple Ashton; Westbury; Tellisford (SOM); Woolverton (SOM); Rode (SOM); Beckington (SOM)
NORTH NEWNTON	Beechingstoke; Wilsford; Rushall; Charlton; Upavon
NORTH WRAXALL	West Kington; Nettleton; Castle Combe; Colerne; Slaughterford; Marshfield (GLS)
NORTH TIDWORTH	Collingbourne Ducis; Ludgershall; Figheldean; Fittleton; South Tidworth (HAM); Kimpton (HAM)
NORTON BAVANT	Edington; Heytesbury; Sutton Veny; Bishopstrow
NORTON COLEPARLE	Sherston Magna; Foxley; Westport St Mary; Hullavington; Grittleton; Grey Easton

NUNTON AND BODENHAM	Odstock; Britford; Alderbury; Downton; Whitsbury

OAKSEY	Kemble; Poole Keynes; Somerford Keynes; Minety; Crudwell
ODSTOCK	Homington; Britford; Nunton and Bodenham; Downton; Whitsbury
OGBOURNE ST GEORGE	Wroughton; Chisledon; Aldbourne; Ramsbury; Mildenhall; Ogbourne St Andrew
OGBOURNE ST ANDREW	Wroughton; Ogbourne St George; Mildenhall; Preshute; Broad Hinton
ORCHESTON ST MARY	Market Lavington; Rushall; Orcheston St George; Tilshead; Charlton
ORCHESTON ST GEORGE	Market Lavington; Rushall; Upavon; Chisenbury; Shrewton; Maddington; Chitterne All Saints; Tilshead; Charlton
OVERTON	Fyfield; Preshute; Huish; Alton Priors; East Kennett; Avebury; Winterbourne Monkton; Savernake; Wilcot

PATNEY	Allcannings; Stanton St Bernard; Beechingstoke; Marden; Chirton; Urchfont; Stert; Etchilhampton
PERTWOOD	Brixton Deverill; Heytesbury; Chicklade; East Knoyle; Monkton Deverill
PEWSEY	Wilcot; Milton Lilborne; Everley; Manningford Abbas
PEWSHAM	Calne; Chittoe; Lacock; Chippenham
PITTON AND FARLEY	Winterbourne Earls; Winterbourne Dauntsey; Winterbourne Gunner; Winterslow; West Dean; West Grimstead; Clarendon Park
PLAITFORD	Melchet Park; West Wellow; Landford; Bramshaw; Whiteparish; Sherfield English (HAM)
POOLE KEYNES	Kemble; Somerford Keynes; Oaksey
PORTON	Idmiston
POTTERNE	Rowde; Devizes St John the Baptist; Bishops Cannings; Etchilhampton; Urchfont; Market Lavington; West Lavington; Little Cheverell; Great Cheverell; Worton and Marston; Keevil; Poulshot; Stert
POULSHOT	Rowde; Potterne; Keevil; Seend
PRESHUTE	Ogbourne St Andrew; Mildenhall; Savernake; Marlborough St Mary the Virgin; Marlborough St Peter & St Paul; Overton; Fyfield; Winterbourne Monkton; Berwick Bassett; Winterbourne Bassett; Broad Hinton
PURTON	Cricklade St Sampson; Blunsdon St Andrew; Rodbourne Cheney; Lydiard Millicent; Brinkworth; Charlton

RAMSBURY	Aldbourne; Baydon; Hungerford; Froxfield; Little Bedwin; Mildenhall; Chilton Foliat; Lambourn (BRK)
RODBOURNE CHENEY	Blunsdon St Andrew; Stratton St Margaret; Swindon; Lydiard Millicent; Purton
ROLLSTONE	Shrewton; Figheldean; Durrington; Winterbourne Stoke; Maddington
ROWDE	Bromham; Bishops Cannings; Devizes St Mary the Virgin; Devizes St John the Baptist; Potterne; Poulshot; Seend; Melksham
RUSHALL	Charlton; North Newnton; Wilsford; Upavon; Chisenbury; Orcheston St George; Orcheston St Mary; Market Lavington

SALISBURY	Fugglestone St Peter with Bemerton; Stratford sub Castle; Milford; Laverstock and Ford; Clarendon Park; Britford; West Harnham
SAVERNAKE	Mildenhall; Little Bedwin; Burbage; Wootton Rivers; Milton Lilborne; Wilcot; Preshute; Easton Royal; Overton
SEAGRY	Malmesbury; Great Somerford; Dauntsey; Christian Malford; Sutton Benger; Stanton St Quintin
SEDGEHILL	Mere; East Knoyle; Tisbury; Semley; Gillingham (DOR); Motcombe (DOR)

SEEND	Melksham; Rowde; Poulshot; Keevil; Semington
SEMINGTON	Melksham; Seend; Keevil; Steeple Ashton; Hilperton; Whaddon
SEMLEY	Sedgehill; Tisbury; Wardour; Donhead St Andrew; Donhead St Mary; Motcombe (DOR)
SEVENHAMPTON	Highworth
SHALBOURNE	Great Bedwin; Little Bedwin; Shalbourne (BRK)
SHERRINGTON	Codford St Peter; Codford St Mary; Stockton; Fonthill Bishop; Berwick St Leonard; Boyton
SHERSTON MAGNA	Sopworth; Grey Easton; Foxley; Norton Coleparle; Hullavington; Alderton; Luckington; Grittleton; Weston Birt (GLS); Tetbury (GLS); Didmarton (GLS); Oldbury on the Hill (GLS)
SHORNCOTE	Somerford Keynes; Ashton Keynes; Siddington (GLS)
SHREWTON	Chisenbury; Enford; Netheravon; Figheldean; Rollstone; Maddington; Orcheston St George; Winterbourne Stoke
SLAUGHTERFORD	Castle Combe; Yatton Keynell; Biddestone; Colerne; North Wraxall
SOMERFORD KEYNES	Kemble; Shorncote; Ashton Keynes; Minety; Oaksey; Poole Keynes; Siddington (GLS)
SOPWORTH	Luckington; Sherston Magna; Didmarton (GLS); Oldbury on the Hill (GLS); Hawkesbury (GLS)
SOUTH WRAXALL	Bradford on Avon
SOUTH MARSTON	Highworth
SOUTH NEWTON	Stapleford; Woodford; Fugglestone St Peter with Bemerton; Wilton; Burcombe; Great Wishford; Durnford
SOUTH DAMERHAM	Martin; Cranbourne (DOR); Rockbourne (HAM)
SOUTHBROOM	Bishops Canning
STANTON ST BERNARD	Allcannings; East Kennett; Alton Barnes; Woodborough; Beechingstoke; Patney; East Kennett
STANTON ST QUINTIN	Grittleton; Hullavington; Malmesbury; Great Somerford; Seagry; Sutton Benger; Draycot Cerne; Kington; Leigh Delamere
STANTON FITZWARREN	Broad Blunsdon; Hannington; Highworth; Stratton St Margaret; Blunsdon St Andrew
STAPLEFORD	Berwick St James; Woodford; South Newton; Great Wishford; Little Langford; Steeple Langford
STAVERTON	Trowbridge; Bradford on Avon; Holt
STEEPLE ASHTON	Hilperton; Semington; Keevil; Edington; Bratton; Westbury; North Bradley; Trowbridge
STEEPLE LANGFORD	Berwick St James; Stapleford; Little Langford; Baverstock; Dinton; Wylye
STERT	Bishops Canning; Patney; Urchfont; Potterne; Etchilhampton
STOCKTON	Codford St Mary; Fisherton Delamere; Chilmark; Fonthill Bishop; Sherrington
STOURTON	Mere; Brewham (SOM); Charlton Musgrave (SOM); Penselwood (SOM)
STRATFORD SUB CASTLE	Durnford; Laverstock and Ford; Milford; Salisbury; Fugglestone St Peter with Bemerton
STRATFORD TONY	Wilton; Netherhampton; Combe Bissett; Martin; Bishopstone
STRATTON ST MARGARET	Blunsdon St Andrew; Stanton Fitzwarren; Highworth; Wanborough; Liddington; Chisledon; Swindon; Rodbourne Cheney
SUTTON MANDEVILLE	Tisbury; Teffont Evias; Fovant; Fifield Bavant; Ebbesbourne Wake; Swallowcliffe
SUTTON BENGER	Seagry; Christian Malford; Bremhill; Langley Burrell; Kington; Draycot Cerne; Stanton St Quintin
SUTTON VENY	Warminster; Bishopstrow; Norton Bavant; Heytesbury; Brixton Deverill; Longbridge Deverill; Hill Deverill
SWALLOWCLIFFE	Tisbury; Sutton Mandeville; Ebbesbourne Wake; Alvediston; Ansty; Wardour
SWINDON	Rodbourne Cheney; Stratton St Margaret; Chisledon; Wroughton; Lydiard Tregoze; Lydiard Millicent

TEFFONT EVIAS	Chilmark; Teffont Magna; Dinton; Fovant; Sutton Mandeville; Tisbury
TEFFONT MAGNA	Fisherton Delamere; Wylye; Dinton; Teffont Evias; Chilmark
TIDCOMBE	Hippenscombe; Buttermere; Chute; Collingbourne Kingston; Great Bedwin; Vernhams Dean (HAM); Shalbourne (BRK)
TILSHEAD	West Lavington; Market Lavington; Orcheston St Mary; Orcheston St George; Maddington; Chitterne All Saints; Imber
TISBURY	Fonthill Gifford; Fonthill Bishop; Chilmark; Teffont Evias; Sutton Mandeville; Swallowcliffe; Wardour; Semley; Sedgehill; East Knoyle
TOCKENHAM	Brinkworth; Wootton Bassett; Cliffe Pypard; Lyneham
TOLLARD ROYAL	Donhead St Mary; Berwick St John; Ashmore (DOR); Tarrant Gonville (DOR); Farnham (DOR); Handley (DOR)
TROWBRIDGE	Bradford on Avon; Hilperton; Steeple Ashton; North Bradley; Staverton
TYTHERTON LUCAS	Chippenham
TYTHERTON KELLAWAYS	Langley Burrell; Christian Malford; Bremhill; Chippenham
UPAVON	Wilsford; Everley; Enford; Chisenbury; Rushall; Orcheston St George; North Newnton
UPTON LOVELL	Knook; Chitterne All Saints; Chitterne St Mary; Codford St Peter; Boyton
UPTON SCUDAMORE	Westbury; Warminster; Corsley; Christchurch
URCHFONT	Stert; Patney; Chirton; Wilsford; Market Lavington; Potterne; Etchilhampton
WANBOROUGH	Little Hinton; Aldbourne; Liddington; Stratton St Margaret; Highworth; Baydon
WARDOUR	Tisbury; Swallowcliffe; Ansty; Donhead St Andrew; Semley
WARMINSTER	Corsley; Upton Scudamore; Westbury; Edington; Bishopstrow; Sutton Veny; Longbridge Deverill; Horningsham; Frome (SOM)
WEST DEAN	Winterslow; Whiteparish; West Grimstead; Pitton and Farley; East Dean (HAM); West Tytherley (HAM); Broughton (HAM); East Tytherley (HAM)
WEST KNOYLE	Kingston Deverill; Monkton Deverill; East Knoyle; Mere
WEST LAVINGTON	Potterne; Market Lavington; Tilshead; Chitterne All Saints; Imber; Little Cheverell
WEST HARNHAM	Fugglestone St Peter with Bemerton; Salisbury; Britford; Coombe Bissett; Netherhampton
WEST GRIMSTEAD	Clarendon Park; Pitton and Farley; West Dean; Whiteparish; Alderbury
WEST KINGTON	Nettleton; North Wraxall; Marshfield (GLS); West Littleton (GLS); Tormarton (GLS)
WEST WELLOW	Plaitford; Bramshaw; Landford; Eling (HAM); East Wellow (HAM); Sherfield English (HAM)
WESTBURY	North Bradley; Steeple Ashton; Edington; Bishopstrow; Warminster; Upton Scudamore; Corsley; Beckington (SOM); Berkley (SOM); Rodden (SOM); Frome (SOM)
WESTPORT ST MARY	Brokenborough; Charlton; Malmesbury; Hullavington; Norton Coleparle; Foxley; Bremilham; Grittleton
WESTWOOD	Bradford on Avon; Wingfield; Freshford (SOM); Hinton Charterhouse (SOM); Farleigh Hungerford (SOM)
WHADDON	Broughton Gifford; Melksham; Semington; Hilperton; Bradford on Avon
WHITEPARISH	West Dean; Melchet Park; Landford; Downton; Alderbury; West Grimstead; Plaitford; East Dean (HAM); Lockerley (HAM); Sherfield English (HAM)
WHITSBURY	Coombe Bissett; Homington; Odstock; Downton; Nunton and Bodenham; Rockbourne (DOR); Breamore (DOR)

WILCOT	Alton Priors; Huish; Savernake; Milton Lilborne; Pewsey; Manningford Abbas; Manningford Bruce; Woodborough; Overton
WILSFORD	Woodborough; Manningford Bruce; Everley; Upavon; Rushall; Charlton; North Newnton; Marden; Market Lavington; Urchfont; Chirton; Beechingstoke
WILSFORD	Amesbury; Durnford; Woodford; Berwick St James; Winterbourne Stoke
WILTON	Burcombe; South Newton; Fugglestone St Peter with Bemerton; Netherhampton; Bishopstone; Stratford Tony
WINGFIELD	Bradford on Avon; Westwood; North Bradley; Farleigh Hungerford (SOM); Tellisford (SOM)
WINSLEY	Bradford on Avon
WINTERBOURNE DAUNTSEY	Durnford; Winterbourne Gunner; Pitton and Farley; Winterbourne Earls
WINTERBOURNE EARLS	Durnford; Winterbourne Dauntsey; Pitton and Farley; Clarendon Park; Laverstock and Ford
WINTERBOURNE GUNNER	Durnford; Idmiston; Winterslow; Pitton and Farley; Winterbourne Dauntsey
WINTERBOURNE MONKTON	Berwick Bassett; Preshute; Overton; Avebury; Yatesbury; Fyfield
WINTERBOURNE STOKE	Rollstone; Durrington; Amesbury; Wilsford; Berwick St James; Maddington; Shrewton
WINTERBOURNE BASSETT	Broad Hinton; Preshute; Berwick Bassett; Cliffe Pypard
WINTERSLOW	Idmiston; Boscombe; West Dean; Pitton and Farley; Winterbourne Gunner; Nether Wallop (HAM); West Tytherley (HAM)
WOODBOROUGH	Stanton St Bernard; Alton Barnes; Alton Priors; Wilcot; Wilsford; Beechingstoke; Manningford Bruce
WOODFORD	Wilsford; Durnford; Fugglestone St Peter with Bemerton; South Newton; Stapleford; Berwick St James
WOOTTON RIVERS	Savernake; Easton Royal; Milton Lilborne
WOOTTON BASSETT	Lydiard Tregoze; Broad Town; Cliffe Pypard; Tockenham; Brinkworth
WORTON AND MARSTON	Keevil; Potterne; Great Cheverell; Erlestoke
WROUGHTON	Lydiard Tregoze; Swindon; Chisledon; Ogbourne St George; Ogbourne St Andrew; Broad Hinton; Broad Town
WYLYE	Maddington; Berwick St James; Steeple Langford; Dinton; Teffont Magna; Fisherton Delamere
YATESBURY	Hilmarton; Berwick Bassett; Avebury; Cherhill; Compton Bassett; Winterbourne Monkton
YATTON KEYNELL	Leigh Delamere; Kington; Chippenham; Biddestone; Slaughterford; Castle Combe